Little Mitchie

ANIMAL ODDBALLS

WEIRD, WILD, AND WONDERFUL

TAMRA B. ORR

CREATING YOUNG NONFICTION READERS

Little Mitchie books spark curiosity and support early nonfiction reading for students in Grades 2-3. Designed to build vocabulary, support second language learners, and prepare readers for middle-grade content, each book includes helpful tips for parents and educators to build confidence and deepen understanding of the world.

TIPS FOR READING NONFICTION WITH BEGINNING READERS

Talk about Nonfiction

Begin by explaining that nonfiction books give us information that is true. The book will be organized around a specific topic or idea, and we may learn new facts through reading.

Look at the Parts

Most nonfiction books have helpful features. Our *Little Mitchie* titles include color photographs and graphic aids, a table of contents, a glossary, and an index. Share the purpose of these features with your reader.

Color Photos and Graphic Aids

A lot of information can be found by "reading" photos, charts, maps, and other graphic aids found within nonfiction texts. Help your reader learn more about the different ways information can be displayed.

Table of Contents

Located at the front of the book, this list shows the big ideas within the text and the page numbers where they can be found.

Glossary

Located at the back of the book, the glossary defines key words and phrases that are related to the topic. These words and phrases can be found in the text in colored type.

Index

Located at the back of the book, an index is an alphabetical list of topics and the page numbers where they can be found.

With a little help and guidance about reading nonfiction, you can feel good about introducing a young reader to the world of *Little Mitchie* nonfiction books.

Little Mitchie is an imprint of:

Mitchell Lane
PUBLISHERS

2001 SW 31st Avenue
Hallandale, FL 33009
mitchelllanepub.com

First Edition, 2027.

Author: Tamra B. Orr
Designer: Jen Bowers
Editor: Tricia Hoffman

Library of Congress Cataloging-in-Publication Data
Title: Animal Oddballs / by Tamra Orr

Description: Hallandale, FL :
Mitchell Lane Publishers, [2027]

Identifiers:
ISBN 979-8-89260-890-9 (library bound)
ISBN 979-8-89260-993-7 (eBook)

Library of Congress Control Number: 2026936383

PHOTO CREDITS
Shutterstock: cover, p.1 ©2025 Logomaker691, p.5 ©2018 Daniel Eskridge, p.7 ©2024 Albert Beukhof, p.8–9 ©2025 hecke61, p.10 ©2015 Andrew M. Allport, p.13 ©2023 Ondrej Prosicky, p.14 ©2009 worldswildlifewonders, p.15 ©2020 Lukas_Vejrik, p.16–17 ©2025 Harsha_Madusanka, p.18 Public Domain/NOAA Ocean Exploration/ Seascape Alaska, p.19 ©2020 Barbara Ash, p.20 ©2016 Ekkapan Poddamrong, p.22 ©2024 NuclearMike, CC BY-SA 4.0 Peter Southwood, ©2019 R.M. Nunes

TABLE OF CONTENTS

Chapter One
ODD ANIMALS . . . 4

Chapter Two
IN THE AIR . . . 6

Chapter Three
ON THE LAND . . . 12

Chapter Four
UNDER THE WATER . . . 18

EVEN WILDER! 22
GLOSSARY . . . 23
FURTHER READING . . . 24
ON THE INTERNET . . . 24
INDEX . . . 24

Chapter One

ODD ANIMALS

There are millions of animals in the world. All of them are wonderful in their own ways. But some are extra weird and wild!

LONG GONE!

Some of the strangest animals are now **extinct**. The glyptodon was a car-sized armadillo. An arthropleura was an eight-foot (2.4-m) millipede!

Chapter Two

IN THE AIR

A shoebill is a weird-looking bird! Found in East Africa, it is as tall as a six-year-old and has an eight-foot (2.4-m) **wingspan**. Its sharp, shoe-shaped bill has a hook at the tip.

Deep in the Amazon jungle lives the hoatzin. It mostly eats leaves. It **digests** slowly, creating very stinky burps! Hoatzin babies have sharp claws on their wings for climbing.

JUNGLE WINGS

More than 10 percent of the bird species in the world are found in the Amazon jungle. More than 1,300 wild species live there, eating insects, fruits, flowers, and other creatures.

Great potoos are night birds. Their huge, bright yellow eyes help them see in the dark. Even when sleeping, they watch for **predators** through eyelid slits. Potoos have wide bills for grabbing insect snacks.

Chapter Three

ON THE LAND

Madagascar is the home of **lemurs** called aye-ayes. They have large eyes, long tails, and teeth that never stop growing. They also have long, bony middle fingers for reaching tasty **grubs**—and for picking their noses!

A SPECIAL PLACE

Madagascar is in the Indian Ocean, off the southeast coast of Africa. Almost all of the animals there are found ONLY there. They include bright red tomato frogs, giant rats, and more than 100 kinds of lemurs.

When tiny glass tree frogs want to sleep, they have to hide from hungry predators in the rainforest. To do so, they send their blood to their liver. This turns their skin as clear as glass and makes them impossible to spot!

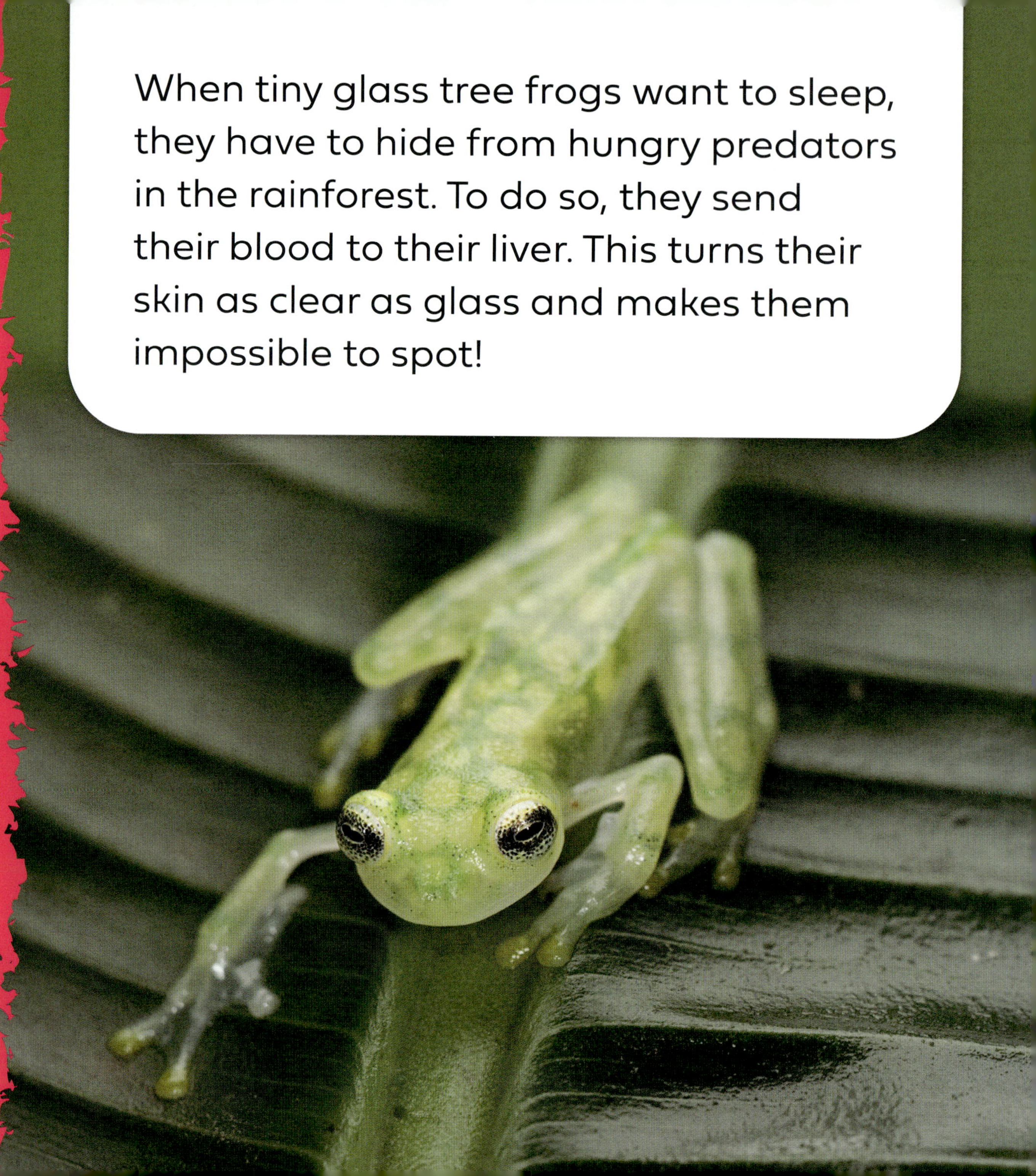

A LITTLE BIT OF EVERYTHING

The platypus is one of nature's oddest animals. It has a duck's bill and webbed feet, but a beaver-like tail and poisonous spurs on its back legs!

In the grasslands of Argentina lives a weird-looking fairy. This tiny creature doesn't have wings, but it does have a pink shell and **silky** white fur. The pink fairy armadillo lives underground and only comes out at night.

Chapter Four

UNDER THE WATER

Oceans are full of weird creatures. The blobfish is one of the weirdest. It looks like a pile of goo oozing along the ocean floor. It moves slowly, but can live more than 100 years!

LIKE A LEAF

Drifting through the oceans around Australia is the leafy seadragon. It looks like just another piece of seaweed passing by. This helps it hide from predators.

Is that a rock? No, it's a decorator crab! This crab hooks algae, sponges, and seaweed to its shell. The decorations help the crab blend in and stay safe from predators.

In the air, on land, or under water, animal oddballs are everywhere!

EVEN WILDER!

The 150-foot (46-m) siphonophore is the longest animal in the world. It looks like a string floating in the water—but beware of its stinging **tentacles**!

The hagfish is an eel-like fish that protects itself by spitting out slime at threats. It can make up to 400 times its own body weight in slime!

Each one of the tarsier's two eyes is bigger than its brain. This primate can turn its head 180 degrees so it can look in all directions.

GLOSSARY

digests (dye-jests) breaks down food into nutrients

extinct (ik-stingkt) having died out, no longer in existence

grubs (gruhbz) the larva of insects

lemurs (lee-murz) small, nocturnal mammals with large eyes, soft fur, and a long tail

predators (pred-uh-turz) animals that live by hunting other animals for food

silky (sil-kee) smooth in texture

tentacles (ten-tuh-kuhlz) long, flexible limbs of some animals that are used to move and to feel and grasp things

wingspan (wing-span) the distance between one end of a wing of a bird and the other

FURTHER READING

Lewis, Jack. *The Weirdest Animals of the World Book for Kids.* Starry Dreamer Publishing, LLC, 2022.

McKay, Sindy. *Very Strange Animals/Animales Muy Extraños.* Treasure Bay, 2025.

ON THE INTERNET

21 Weirdest Animals
www.discoverwildlife.com/animal-facts/weird-animals
Check out 21 of the world's must unusual animals, both on land and in the ocean.

The Ocean's Weirdest Creatures!
www.natgeokids.com/uk/discover/animals/sea-life/strange-sea-creatures/
Get ready to meet some of the ocean's strangest creatures!

INDEX

bill 6, 11
extinct 5
eyes 11, 12, 22
jungle 8, 9
ocean 13, 18, 19
predators 11, 14, 19, 21
rainforest 14
wings 8, 16